This collection of 9 home and fashion accessories from designer Kristi Simpson will inspire your creative side. Crocheted with shades of solid gradient colors or with self-striping yarns, they will color your world beautiful!

CONTENTS

LEISURE ARTS, INC. • Maumelle, Arkansas

●●○○ EASY

LACY WRAP

Finished Size: Approximately 21½" x 48" (54.5 cm x 122 cm) (excluding Flowers)

SHOPPING LIST

Yarn (Medium Weight) MEDIUM 4

[3.5 ounces, 175 yards (100 grams, 160 meters) per skein]:

- ☐ Grey - 1 skein
- ☐ Cream - 1 skein
- ☐ Pink - 1 skein

Crochet Hook

- ☐ Size M/N (9 mm) **or** size needed for gauge

GAUGE INFORMATION

In pattern, sc, (ch 5, sc) twice and Rows 1-5 = 4½" (11.5 cm)

Gauge Swatch: 2½" (6.25 cm) diameter

Work same as Flower: 5 petals.

FLOWER (Make 13)

Rnd 1 (Right side)**:** With Pink, ch 2, 5 sc in second ch from hook; join with slip st to first sc.

Note: Loop a short piece of yarn around any stitch to mark Rnd 1 as **right** side.

Rnd 2: Ch 1, (2 dc, ch 1, slip st) in same st as joining, (slip st, ch 1, 2 dc, ch 1, slip st) in each sc around; join with slip st to joining slip st, finish off: 5 petals.

WRAP

With Grey, ch 131.

Row 1: Working in back ridges of beginning ch ***(Fig. 1, page 29)***, sc in second ch from hook, ch 5, ★ skip next 3 chs, sc in next 2 chs, ch 5; repeat from ★ across to last 4 chs, skip next 3 chs, sc in last ch: 26 ch-5 sps.

Row 2 (Right side)**:** Ch 5 **(counts as first dc plus ch 2, now and thoughout)**, turn; sc in next ch-5 sp, (ch 5, sc in next ch-5 sp) across to last sc, ch 2, dc in last sc: 27 sps.

Note: Mark Row 2 as **right** side.

Row 3: Ch 1, turn; sc in first dc, ch 3, skip next ch-2 sp, (2 sc in next ch-5 sp, ch 3) across to last ch-2 sp, skip last ch-2 sp, sc in last dc: 26 ch-3 sps.

Row 4: Ch 5, turn; sc in next ch-3 sp, (ch 5, sc in next ch-3 sp) across to last sc, ch 2, dc in last sc: 27 sps.

Rows 5-12: Repeat Rows 3 and 4, 4 times; at end of Row 12, finish off.

Row 13: With **wrong** side facing, join Cream with sc in first dc ***(see Joining With Sc, page 29)***; ch 3, skip next ch-2 sp, (2 sc in next ch-5 sp, ch 3) across to last ch-2 sp, skip last ch-2 sp, sc in last dc: 26 ch-3 sps.

Row 14: Ch 5, turn; sc in next ch-3 sp, (ch 5, sc in next ch-3 sp) across to last sc, ch 2, dc in last sc: 27 sps.

Rows 15-20: Repeat Rows 3 and 4, 3 times; at end of Row 20, finish off.

Rows 21-23: With Pink, repeat Rows 13-15: 26 ch-3 sps.

Row 24 (Joining row)**:** Ch 5, turn; sc in next ch-3 sp, ch 2, with **wrong** sides of Wrap and first Flower together, slip st in sp **between** 2 dc on any petal ***(Fig. 6, page 30)***, ch 2, sc in next ch-3 sp, ★ ch 5, sc in next ch-3 sp, ch 2, with **wrong** sides of Wrap and next Flower together, slip st in sp **between** 2 dc on any petal, ch 2, sc in next ch-3 sp; repeat from ★ across to last sc, ch 2, dc in last sc; finish off.

●●○○ EASY

Finished Size:
6" wide x 65" long
(15.25 cm x 165 cm)

SIMPLE SCARF

SHOPPING LIST

Yarn (Light Weight) LIGHT 3

[5.3 ounces, 590 yards
(150 grams, 540 meters) per skein]:

- ☐ 1 skein

Crochet Hook

- ☐ Size H (5 mm)
  or size needed for gauge

GAUGE INFORMATION

In pattern,
15 dc and 9 rows = 4" (10 cm)
Gauge Swatch: 6" wide x 4" high
(15.25 cm x 10 cm)
Work same as Scarf for 9 rows: 23 dc.

SCARF

Ch 24.

Row 1: Working in back ridges of beginning ch ***(Fig. 1, page 29)***, sc in second ch from hook and in each ch across: 23 sc.

Row 2 (Right side)**:** Ch 3 **(counts as first dc, now and throughout)**, turn; ★ dc in next 2 sc, dc **around** last 2 dc made ***(Fig. A)***, skip next sc; repeat from ★ across to last sc, dc in last sc.

Fig. A

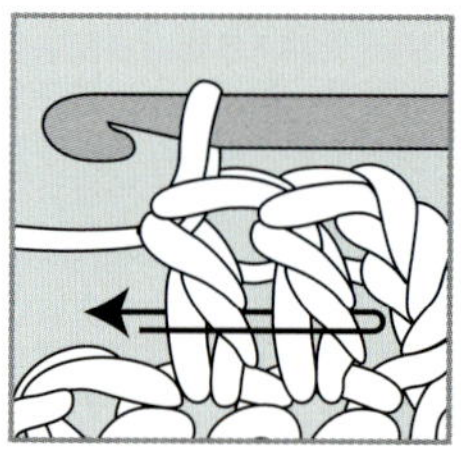

Row 3: Ch 3, turn; dc in next dc and in each dc across.

Row 4: Ch 1, turn; sc in first dc, ch 3, ★ skip next 2 dc, sc in next dc, ch 3; repeat from ★ across to last 4 dc, skip next 2 dc, sc in last 2 dc: 9 sc and 7 ch-3 sps.

Row 5: Ch 3, turn; ★ skip next sc, 2 dc in next ch-3 sp, dc **around** last 2 dc made; repeat from ★ across to last sc, dc in last sc: 23 dc.

Repeat Rows 3-5 for pattern until Scarf measures approximately 65" (165 cm) from beginning ch, ending by working Row 5.

Last Row: Ch 1, turn; sc in each dc across; finish off.

●●○○ EASY

Finished Size: 60" (152.5 cm) diameter

STAR BLANKET

SHOPPING LIST

Yarn (Medium Weight) MEDIUM 4

[3.5 ounces, 175 yards (100 grams, 160 meters) per skein]:

- ☐ Black - 3 skeins
- ☐ Green - 2 skeins
- ☐ Lt Grey - 2 skeins
- ☐ Dk Grey - 2 skeins
- ☐ Cream - 1 skein

Crochet Hook

- ☐ Size J (6 mm) **or** size needed for gauge

GAUGE INFORMATION

10 dc and 7 rnds = 4" (10 cm)

Gauge Swatch: 3½" (9 cm) diameter

Work same as Blanket through Rnd 2: 24 dc.

BLANKET

With Cream, ch 4; join with slip st to form a ring.

Rnd 1 (Right side)**:** Ch 3 **(counts as first dc, now and throughout)**, 11 dc in ring; join with slip st to first dc: 12 dc.

Note: Loop a short piece of yarn around any stitch to mark Rnd 1 as **right** side.

Rnd 2: Ch 3, dc in same st as joining, 2 dc in next dc and in each dc around; join with slip st to first dc: 24 dc.

Rnd 3: Ch 5 **(counts as first dc plus ch 2)**, dc in same st as joining, skip next dc, ★ (dc, ch 2, dc) in next dc, skip next dc; repeat from ★ around; join with slip st to first dc: 24 dc and 12 ch-2 sps.

Rnd 4: Slip st in next ch-2 sp, ch 3, (dc, ch 2, 2 dc) in same sp, (2 dc, ch 2, 2 dc) in each ch-2 sp around; join with slip st to first dc: 48 dc and 12 ch-2 sps.

Rnd 5: Slip st in next dc, ch 3, (2 dc, ch 2, 2 dc) in next ch-2 sp, dc in next dc, ★ skip next 2 dc, dc in next dc, (2 dc, ch 2, 2 dc) in next ch-2 sp, dc in next dc; repeat from ★ around to last 2 sts, skip last 2 sts; join with slip st to first dc: 72 dc and 12 ch-2 sps.

Rnd 6: Slip st in next dc, ch 3, dc in next dc, (2 dc, ch 2, 2 dc) in next ch-2 sp, dc in next 2 dc, ★ skip next 2 dc, dc in next 2 dc, (2 dc, ch 2, 2 dc) in next ch-2 sp, dc in next 2 dc; repeat from ★ around to last 2 sts, skip last 2 sts; join with slip st to first dc: 96 dc and 12 ch-2 sps.

Rnd 7: Slip st in next dc, ch 3, dc in next 2 dc, (2 dc, ch 2, 2 dc) in next ch-2 sp, dc in next 3 dc, ★ skip next 2 dc, dc in next 3 dc, (2 dc, ch 2, 2 dc) in next ch-2 sp, dc in next 3 dc; repeat from ★ around to last 2 sts, skip last 2 sts; join with slip st to first dc: 120 dc and 12 ch-2 sps.

Rnd 8: Slip st in next dc, ch 3, dc in next 3 dc, (dc, ch 2, dc) in next ch-2 sp, dc in next 4 dc, ★ skip next 2 dc, dc in next 4 dc, (dc, ch 2, dc) in next ch-2 sp, dc in next 4 dc; repeat from ★ around to last 2 sts, skip last 2 sts; join with slip st to first dc.

Rnd 9: Slip st in next dc, ch 3, dc in next 3 dc, (2 dc, ch 2, 2 dc) in next ch-2 sp, dc in next 4 dc, ★ skip next 2 dc, dc in next 4 dc, (2 dc, ch 2, 2 dc) in next ch-2 sp, dc in next 4 dc; repeat from ★ around to last 2 sts, skip last 2 sts; join with slip st to first dc, finish off: 144 dc and 12 ch-2 sps.

Rnd 10: With **right** side facing, skip first dc and join Green with slip st in next dc; ch 3, dc in next 4 dc, (dc, ch 2, dc) in next ch-2 sp, dc in next 5 dc, ★ skip next 2 dc, dc in next 5 dc, (dc, ch 2, dc) in next ch-2 sp, dc in next 5 dc; repeat from ★ around to last 2 sts, skip last 2 sts; join with slip st to first dc, finish off.

Rnd 11: With **right** side facing, skip first dc and join Cream with slip st in next dc; ch 3, dc in next 4 dc, (2 dc, ch 2, 2 dc) in next ch-2 sp, dc in next 5 dc, ★ skip next 2 dc, dc in next 5 dc, (2 dc, ch 2, 2 dc) in next ch-2 sp, dc in next 5 dc; repeat from ★ around to last 2 sts, skip last 2 sts; join with slip st to first dc, finish off: 168 dc and 12 ch-2 sps.

Rnd 12: With **right** side facing, skip first dc and join Green with slip st in next dc, ch 3; dc in next 5 dc, (dc, ch 2, dc) in next ch-2 sp, dc in next 6 dc, ★ skip next 2 dc, dc in next 6 dc, (dc, ch 2, dc) in next ch-2 sp, dc in next 6 dc; repeat from ★ around to last 2 sts, skip last 2 sts; join with slip st to first dc.

Rnd 13: Slip st in next dc, ch 3, dc in next 5 dc, (2 dc, ch 2, 2 dc) in next ch-2 sp, dc in next 6 dc, ★ skip next 2 dc, dc in next 6 dc, (2 dc, ch 2, 2 dc) in next ch-2 sp, dc in next 6 dc; repeat from ★ around to last 2 sts, skip last 2 sts; join with slip st to first dc: 192 dc and 12 ch-2 sps.

Rnd 14: Slip st in next dc, ch 3, dc in next 6 dc, (dc, ch 2, dc) in next ch-2 sp, dc in next 7 dc, ★ skip next 2 dc, dc in next 7 dc, (dc, ch 2, dc) in next ch-2 sp, dc in next 7 dc; repeat from ★ around to last 2 sts, skip last 2 sts; join with slip st to first dc.

Rnd 15: Slip st in next dc, ch 3, dc in next 6 dc, (2 dc, ch 2, 2 dc) in next ch-2 sp, dc in next 7 dc, ★ skip next 2 dc, dc in next 7 dc, (2 dc, ch 2, 2 dc) in next ch-2 sp, dc in next 7 dc; repeat from ★ around to last 2 sts, skip last 2 sts; join with slip st to first dc: 216 dc and 12 ch-2 sps.

Rnd 16: Slip st in next dc, ch 3, dc in next 7 dc, (dc, ch 2, dc) in next ch-2 sp, dc in next 8 dc, ★ skip next 2 dc, dc in next 8 dc, (dc, ch 2, dc) in next ch-2 sp, dc in next 8 dc; repeat from ★ around to last 2 sts, skip last 2 sts; join with slip st to first dc, finish off.

Rnd 17: With **right** side facing, skip first dc and join Lt Grey with slip st in next dc; ch 3, dc in next 7 dc, (2 dc, ch 2, 2 dc) in next ch-2 sp, dc in next 8 dc, ★ skip next 2 dc, dc in next 8 dc, (2 dc, ch 2, 2 dc) in next ch-2 sp, dc in next 8 dc; repeat from ★ around to last 2 sts, skip last 2 sts; join with slip st to first dc, finish off: 240 dc and 12 ch-2 sps.

Rnd 18: With **right** side facing, skip first dc and join Green with slip st in next dc; ch 3, dc in next 8 dc, (dc, ch 2, dc) in next ch-2 sp, dc in next 9 dc, ★ skip next 2 dc, dc in next 9 dc, (dc, ch 2, dc) in next ch-2 sp, dc in next 9 dc; repeat from ★ around to last 2 sts, skip last 2 sts; join with slip st to first dc, finish off.

Rnd 19: With **right** side facing, skip first dc and join Lt Grey with slip st in next dc; ch 3, dc in next 8 dc, (2 dc, ch 2, 2 dc) in next ch-2 sp, dc in next 9 dc, ★ skip next 2 dc, dc in next 9 dc, (2 dc, ch 2, 2 dc) in next ch-2 sp, dc in next 9 dc; repeat from ★ around to last 2 sts, skip last 2 sts; join with slip st to first dc: 264 dc and 12 ch-2 sps.

Rnd 20: Slip st in next dc, ch 3, dc in next 9 dc, (dc, ch 2, dc) in next ch-2 sp, dc in next 10 dc, ★ skip next 2 dc, dc in next 10 dc, (dc, ch 2, dc) in next ch-2 sp, dc in next 10 dc; repeat from ★ around to last 2 sts, skip last 2 sts; join with slip st to first dc.

Rnd 21: Slip st in next dc, ch 3, dc in next 9 dc, (2 dc, ch 2, 2 dc) in next ch-2 sp, dc in next 10 dc, ★ skip next 2 dc, dc in next 10 dc, (2 dc, ch 2, 2 dc) in next ch-2 sp, dc in next 10 dc; repeat from ★ around to last 2 sts, skip last 2 sts; join with slip st to first dc: 288 dc and 12 ch-2 sps.

Rnd 22: Slip st in next dc, ch 3, dc in next 10 dc, (dc, ch 2, dc) in next ch-2 sp, dc in next 11 dc, ★ skip next 2 dc, dc in next 11 dc, (dc, ch 2, dc) in next ch-2 sp, dc in next 11 dc; repeat from ★ around to last 2 sts, skip last 2 sts; join with slip st to first dc.

Rnd 23: Slip st in next dc, ch 3, dc in next 10 dc, (2 dc, ch 2, 2 dc) in next ch-2 sp, dc in next 11 dc, ★ skip next 2 dc, dc in next 11 dc, (2 dc, ch 2, 2 dc) in next ch-2 sp, dc in next 11 dc; repeat from ★ around to last 2 sts, skip last 2 sts; join with slip st to first dc, finish off: 312 dc and 12 ch-2 sps.

Rnd 24: With **right** side facing, skip first dc and join Dk Grey with slip st in next dc; ch 3, dc in next 11 dc, (dc, ch 2, dc) in next ch-2 sp, dc in next 12 dc, ★ skip next 2 dc, dc in next 12 dc, (dc, ch 2, dc) in next ch-2 sp, dc in next 12 dc; repeat from ★ around to last 2 sts, skip last 2 sts; join with slip st to first dc, finish off.

Rnd 25: With **right** side facing, skip first dc and join Lt Grey with slip st in next dc; ch 3, dc in next 11 dc, (2 dc, ch 2, 2 dc) in next ch-2 sp, dc in next 12 dc, ★ skip next 2 dc, dc in next 12 dc, (2 dc, ch 2, 2 dc) in next ch-2 sp, dc in next 12 dc; repeat from ★ around to last 2 sts, skip last 2 sts; join with slip st to first dc, finish off: 336 dc and 12 ch-2 sps.

Rnd 26: With **right** side facing, skip first dc and join Dk Grey with slip st in next dc; ch 3, dc in next 12 dc, (dc, ch 2, dc) in next ch-2 sp, dc in next 13 dc, ★ skip next 2 dc, dc in next 13 dc, (dc, ch 2, dc) in next ch-2 sp, dc in next 13 dc; repeat from ★ around to last 2 sts, skip last 2 sts; join with slip st to first dc.

Rnd 27: Slip st in next dc, ch 3, dc in next 12 dc, (2 dc, ch 2, 2 dc) in next ch-2 sp, dc in next 13 dc, ★ skip next 2 dc, dc in next 13 dc, (2 dc, ch 2, 2 dc) in next ch-2 sp, dc in next 13 dc; repeat from ★ around to last 2 sts, skip last 2 sts; join with slip st to first dc: 360 dc and 12 ch-2 sps.

Rnd 28: Slip st in next dc, ch 3, dc in next 13 dc, (dc, ch 2, dc) in next ch-2 sp, dc in next 14 dc, ★ skip next 2 dc, dc in next 14 dc, (dc, ch 2, dc) in next ch-2 sp, dc in next 14 dc; repeat from ★ around to last 2 sts, skip last 2 sts; join with slip st to first dc.

Rnd 29: Slip st in next dc, ch 3, dc in next 13 dc, (2 dc, ch 2, 2 dc) in next ch-2 sp, dc in next 14 dc, ★ skip next 2 dc, dc in next 14 dc, (2 dc, ch 2, 2 dc) in next ch-2 sp, dc in next 14 dc; repeat from ★ around to last 2 sts, skip last 2 sts; join with slip st to first dc: 384 dc and 12 ch-2 sps.

Rnd 30: Slip st in next dc, ch 3, dc in next 14 dc, (dc, ch 2, dc) in next ch-2 sp, dc in next 15 dc, ★ skip next 2 dc, dc in next 15 dc, (dc, ch 2, dc) in next ch-2 sp, dc in next 15 dc; repeat from ★ around to last 2 sts, skip last 2 sts; join with slip st to first dc, finish off.

Rnd 31: With **right** side facing, skip first dc and join Black with slip st in next dc; ch 3, dc in next 14 dc, (2 dc, ch 2, 2 dc) in next ch-2 sp, dc in next 15 dc, ★ skip next 2 dc, dc in next 15 dc, (2 dc, ch 2, 2 dc) in next ch-2 sp, dc in next 15 dc; repeat from ★ around to last 2 sts, skip last 2 sts; join with slip st to first dc, finish off: 408 dc and 12 ch-2 sps.

Rnd 32: With **right** side facing, skip first dc and join Dk Grey with slip st in next dc; ch 3, dc in next 15 dc, (dc, ch 2, dc) in next ch-2 sp, dc in next 16 dc, ★ skip next 2 dc, dc in next 16 dc, (dc, ch 2, dc) in next ch-2 sp, dc in next 16 dc; repeat from ★ around to last 2 sts, skip last 2 sts; join with slip st to first dc, finish off.

Rnd 33: With **right** side facing, skip first dc and join Black with slip st in next dc; ch 3, dc in next 15 dc, (2 dc, ch 2, 2 dc) in next ch-2 sp, dc in next 16 dc, ★ skip next 2 dc, dc in next 16 dc, (2 dc, ch 2, 2 dc) in next ch-2 sp, dc in next 16 dc; repeat from ★ around to last 2 sts, skip last 2 sts; join with slip st to first dc: 432 dc and 12 ch-2 sps.

Rnd 34: Slip st in next dc, ch 3, dc in next 16 dc, (dc, ch 2, dc) in next ch-2 sp, dc in next 17 dc, ★ skip next 2 dc, dc in next 17 dc, (dc, ch 2, dc) in next ch-2 sp, dc in next 17 dc; repeat from ★ around to last 2 sts, skip last 2 sts; join with slip st to first dc.

Rnd 35: Slip st in next dc, ch 3, dc in next 16 dc, (2 dc, ch 2, 2 dc) in next ch-2 sp, dc in next 17 dc, ★ skip next 2 dc, dc in next 17 dc, (2 dc, ch 2, 2 dc) in next ch-2 sp, dc in next 17 dc; repeat from ★ around to last 2 sts, skip last 2 sts; join with slip st to first dc: 456 dc and 12 ch-2 sps.

Rnd 36: Slip st in next dc, ch 1, sc in same st and in next 17 dc, 3 sc in next ch-2 sp, sc in next 18 dc, ★ skip next 2 dc, sc in next 18 dc, 3 sc in next ch-2 sp, sc in next 18 dc; repeat from ★ around to last 2 sts, skip last 2 sts; join with slip st to first sc, finish off.

SLOUCHY HAT

●●○○ EASY

Finished Size:
Fits 20-22" (51-56 cm) head circumference

Shown on page 12.

SHOPPING LIST

Yarn (Medium Weight) MEDIUM 4

[1.4 ounces, 72 yards (40 grams, 66 meters) per skein]:

- ☐ Dk Teal - 1 skein
- ☐ Teal - 1 skein
- ☐ Green - 1 skein
- ☐ Lt Green - 1 skein
- ☐ Pale Green - 1 skein

Crochet Hook

- ☐ Size H (5 mm)
  or size needed for gauge

Additional Supplies

- ☐ Yarn needle

GAUGE INFORMATION

13 dc and 7 rows/rnds = 4" (10 cm)

Gauge Swatch: 4" (10 cm) square

Ch 15.

Row 1: Dc in fourth ch from hook **(3 skipped chs count as first dc)** and in each ch across: 13 dc.

Rows 2-7: Ch 3 **(counts as first dc)**, turn; dc in next dc and in each dc across.

Finish off.

STITCH GUIDE

BACK POST DOUBLE CROCHET ***(abbreviated BPdc)***

YO, insert hook from **back** to **front** around post of st indicated ***(Fig. 4, page 29)***, YO and pull up a loop (3 loops on hook), (YO and draw through 2 loops on hook) twice.

FRONT POST DOUBLE CROCHET ***(abbreviated FPdc)***

YO, insert hook from **front** to **back** around post of st indicated ***(Fig. 4, page 29)***, YO and pull up a loop (3 loops on hook), (YO and draw through 2 loops on hook) twice.

LONG DC ***(abbreviated LDC)***

YO, working **around** next dc, insert hook in ch-1 sp one row **below** ***(Fig. 7, page 30)***, YO and pull up a loop even with last st made (3 loops on hook), (YO and draw through 2 loops on hook) twice.

BAND

Leaving a long end for sewing, with Dk Teal, ch 61.

Rnd 1 (Right side)**:** Working in back ridges of beginning ch ***(Fig. 1, page 29)***, sc in second ch from hook and in each ch across; being careful **not** to twist piece, join with slip st to first sc: 60 sc.

Note: Loop a short piece of yarn around any stitch to mark Rnd 1 as **right** side.

Rnd 2: Ch 2 (does **not** count as a st), work FPdc around same st as joining and around next sc, work BPdc around each of next 2 sc, ★ work FPdc around each of next 2 sc, work BPdc around each of next 2 sc; repeat from ★ around; join with slip st to first FPdc.

Rnds 3 and 4: Ch 2 (does **not** count as a st), work FPdc around same st as joining and around next FPdc, work BPdc around each of next 2 BPdc, ★ work FPdc around each of next 2 FPdc, work BPdc around each of next 2 BPdc; repeat from ★ around; join with slip st to first FPdc.

Finish off.

BODY

Rnd 1: With **right** side facing, join Teal with dc in first FPdc *(see Joining With Dc, page 29)*; dc in next 2 sts, ch 1, skip next BPdc, ★ dc in next 3 sts, ch 1, skip next BPdc; repeat from ★ around; join with slip st to first dc: 45 dc and 15 ch-1 sps.

Rnd 2: Ch 3 **(counts as first dc, now and throughout)**, dc in next 2 dc and in next ch-1 sp, (dc in next 3 dc and next ch-1 sp) around; join with slip st to first dc, finish off: 60 dc.

Rnd 3: With **right** side facing, skip first 2 dc and join Green with dc in next dc; work LDC, dc in next dc, ch 1, skip next dc, ★ dc in next dc, work LDC, dc in next dc, ch 1, skip next dc; repeat from ★ around; join with slip st to first dc: 45 sts and 15 ch-1 sps.

Rnd 4: Ch 3, dc in next 2 sts and in next ch-1 sp, (dc in next 3 sts and in next ch-1 sp) around; join with slip st to first dc, finish off: 60 dc.

Rnd 5: With **right** side facing, join Lt Green with dc in next-to-last dc of previous rnd; work LDC, dc in next dc, ch 1, skip next dc, ★ dc in next dc, work LDC, dc in next dc, ch 1, skip next dc; repeat from ★ around; join with slip st to first dc: 45 sts and 15 ch-1 sps.

Rnd 6: Ch 3, dc in next 2 sts and in next ch-1 sp, (dc in next 3 sts and in next ch-1 sp) around; join with slip st to first dc, finish off: 60 dc.

Rnds 7 and 8: With Pale Green, repeat Rnds 3 and 4: 60 dc.

Rnds 9 and 10: With Teal, repeat Rnds 5 and 6: 60 dc.

Rnds 11-13: Repeat Rnds 3-5: 45 sts and 15 ch-1 sps.

Rnd 14: Ch 3, dc in next 2 sts and in next ch-1 sp, (dc in next 3 sts and in next ch-1 sp) around; join with slip st to first dc, finish off leaving a long end for sewing: 60 dc.

FINISHING

Turn piece **wrong** side out and sew top of Hat closed as follows: Using scrap pieces of yarn, pins, or split-ring markers, place 8 markers evenly spaced around top of hat, having first marker where long end is attached to piece. Thread yarn needle with long end. Following diagram, sew through fabric at 2, bringing 1 and 2 together at center. Continue sewing through marked areas numerically, having each meet at center; secure end.

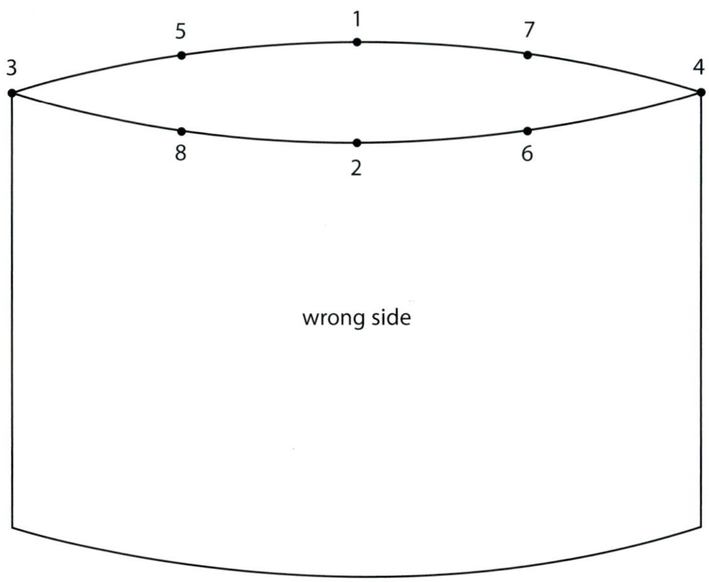

Thread yarn needle with beginning end and sew through chs at base of first and last sc; secure end.

TRIANGLE SHAWL

●●○○ EASY

Finished Size:

54½" long x 13¼" wide at point (138.5 cm x 33.5 cm)

SHOPPING LIST

Yarn (Medium Weight) MEDIUM 4

[5 ounces, 280 yards (140 grams, 256 meters) per skein**]**:

☐ 2 skeins

Crochet Hook

☐ Size H (5 mm)
or size needed for gauge

GAUGE INFORMATION

In pattern,
13 sts and 9 rows = 4" (10 cm)

Gauge Swatch: 4" (10 cm) square

Ch 14.

Row 1: Hdc in second ch from hook and in each ch across: 13 hdc.

Row 2: Ch 1, turn; hdc in first hdc and in each hdc across.

Row 3: Ch 4 **(counts as first dc plus ch 1)**, turn; skip next hdc, dc in next hdc, (ch 1, skip next hdc, dc in next hdc) across: 7 dc and 6 ch-1 sps.

Row 4: Ch 1, turn; hdc in first dc, (hdc in next ch-1 sp and in next dc) across: 13 hdc.

Rows 5-9: Repeat Rows 2-4 once, then repeat Rows 2 and 3 once **more**. Finish off.

STITCH GUIDE

BEGINNING HALF DOUBLE CROCHET 2 TOGETHER *(abbreviated beginning hdc2tog)*
(uses first st and next ch-1 sp)
YO, insert hook in first st, YO and pull up a loop, YO, insert hook in next ch-1 sp, YO and pull up a loop, YO and draw through all 5 loops on hook **(counts as first hdc)**.

HALF DOUBLE CROCHET 2 TOGETHER *(abbreviated hdc2tog)*
(uses next 2 sts **or** next sp and last dc)
(YO, insert hook in **next** st or sp, YO and pull up a loop) twice, YO and draw through all 5 loops on hook **(counts as one hdc)**.

SHAWL

Ch 3.

Row 1: Hdc in second ch from hook and in last ch: 2 hdc.

Row 2 (Right side)**:** Ch 2 (does **not** count as a st), turn; 2 hdc in first hdc, hdc in last hdc: 3 hdc.

Row 3: Ch 3 **(counts as first dc)**, turn; dc in next 2 hdc.

Row 4: Ch 1, turn; 2 hdc in first dc, hdc last 2 dc: 4 hdc.

Row 5: Ch 1, turn; hdc in first 3 hdc, 2 hdc in last hdc: 5 hdc.

Row 6: Ch 4 **(counts as first dc plus ch 1, now and throughout)**, turn; skip next hdc, dc in next hdc, ch 1, skip next hdc, dc in last hdc: 3 dc and 2 ch-1 sps.

Row 7: Ch 1, turn; hdc in first dc and in next ch-1 sp, hdc in next dc and in next ch-1 sp, 2 hdc in last dc: 6 hdc.

Row 8: Ch 1, turn; 2 hdc in first hdc, hdc in each hdc across: 7 hdc.

Row 9: Ch 4, turn; skip next hdc, dc in next hdc, (ch 1, skip next hdc, dc in next hdc) across: 4 dc and 3 ch-1 sps.

Row 10: Ch 1, turn; 2 hdc in first dc, (hdc in next ch-1 sp and in next dc) across: 8 hdc.

Row 11: Ch 1, turn; hdc in first hdc and in each hdc across to last hdc, 2 hdc in last hdc: 9 hdc.

Row 12: Ch 4, turn; skip next hdc, dc in next hdc, (ch 1, skip next hdc, dc in next hdc) across: 5 dc and 4 ch-1 sps.

Row 13: Ch 1, turn; hdc in first dc and in next ch-1 sp, (hdc in next dc and in next ch-1 sp) across to last dc, 2 hdc in last dc: 10 hdc.

Rows 14-63: Repeat Rows 8-13, 8 times; then repeat Rows 8 and 9 once **more**: 22 dc and 21 ch-1 sps.

Row 64: Ch 1, turn; work beginning hdc2tog, hdc in next dc, (hdc in next ch-1 sp and in next dc) across: 42 hdc.

Row 65: Ch 1, turn; hdc in first hdc and in each hdc across to last 2 hdc, hdc2tog: 41 hdc.

Row 66: Ch 4, turn; skip next hdc, dc in next hdc, (ch 1, skip next hdc, dc in next hdc) across: 21 dc and 20 ch-1 sps.

Row 67: Ch 1, turn; hdc in first dc, (hdc in next ch-1 sp and in next dc) across to last ch-1 sp, hdc2tog: 40 hdc.

Row 68: Ch 1, turn; work beginning hdc2tog, hdc in each hdc across: 39 hdc.

Row 69: Ch 4, turn; skip next hdc, dc in next hdc, (ch 1, skip next hdc, dc in next hdc) across: 20 dc and 19 ch-1 sps.

Rows 70-120: Repeat Rows 64-69, 8 times; then repeat Rows 64-66 once **more**: 3 dc and 2 ch-1 sps.

Row 121: Ch 1, turn; hdc in first dc, hdc in next ch-1 sp and in next dc, hdc2tog: 4 hdc.

Row 122: Ch 1, turn; work beginning hdc2tog, hdc in last 2 hdc: 3 hdc.

Row 123: Ch 1, turn; hdc in first hdc, hdc2tog; finish off.

SWEET TOTE

●●○○ EASY

Finished Size:
10½"w x 10"h (26.5 cm x 25.5 cm)
(excluding Straps)

Shown on page 18.

SHOPPING LIST

Yarn (Medium Weight) MEDIUM 4
[10 ounces, 482 yards
(283 grams, 440 meters) per skein]:
- ☐ 1 skein

Crochet Hook
- ☐ Size H (5 mm)
  or size needed for gauge

Additional Supplies
- ☐ Yarn needle

GAUGE INFORMATION

In pattern, 13 sts and 11 rows/rnds = 4" (10 cm)

Gauge Swatch: 4" (10 cm) square

Ch 14.

Row 1: Sc in second ch from hook and in each ch across: 13 sc.

Row 2: Ch 1, turn; sc in first sc, ★ ch 1, skip next st, sc in next sc; repeat from ★ across: 7 sc and 6 ch-1 sps.

Row 3: Ch 1, turn; sc in first sc, (dc in next ch-1 sp, sc in next sc) across: 13 sts.

Rows 4-11: Repeat Rows 2 and 3, 4 times.

Finish off.

STITCH GUIDE

TREBLE CROCHET ***(abbreviated tr)***

YO twice, insert hook in ch indicated, YO and pull up a loop (4 loops on hook), (YO and draw through 2 loops on hook) 3 times.

BASE

Ch 31.

Row 1 (Right side)**:** Sc in the second ch from the hook and in each ch across: 30 sc.

Note: Loop a short piece of yarn around any stitch to mark Row 1 as **right** side.

Rows 2-5: Ch 1, turn; sc in each sc across; at end of Row 5, do **not** finish off.

SIDES

Rnd 1: Ch 1, do **not** turn; sc in end of same row and each row across, working in free loops of beginning ch ***(Fig. 2, page 29)***, sc in each ch across ending in ch at base of first sc; sc in end of each row across; sc in each sc across Row 5; join with slip st to first sc: 70 sc.

Rnd 2: Ch 1, sc in same st as joining, ch 1, skip next st, ★ sc in next sc, ch 1, skip next st; repeat from ★ around; join with slip st to first sc: 35 sc and 35 ch-1 sps.

Rnd 3: Ch 1, sc in same st as joining, dc in next ch-1 sp, (sc in next sc, dc in next ch-1 sp) around; join with slip st to first sc: 70 sts.

Rnds 4-27: Repeat Rnds 2 and 3, 12 times.

Rnd 28: Ch 1; working from **left** to **right**, work reverse sc in each st around ***(Figs. 5a-d, page 30)***; join with slip st to first st, finish off.

STRAP (Make 2)

Ch 56.

Row 1 (Wrong side)**:** Working in back ridges of beginning ch ***(Fig. 1, page 29)***, sc in second ch from hook and in each ch across: 55 sc.

Note: Mark **back** of any stitch on Row 1 as **right** side.

Rows 2-4: Ch 1, turn; sc in each sc across.

Finish off.

With **right** sides facing and using photo as a guide for placement, sew one Strap to each side of Tote.

FLOWER

Ch 23.

Row 1: Tr in third ch from hook and in next 7 chs, 2 dc in each of next 6 chs, 3 sc in each of last 7 chs; finish off leaving a 10" (25.5 cm) end for sewing.

With sc end at center, roll up beginning ch edge to form Flower. Thread yarn needle with long end and tack base of Flower in place; secure end, do **not** cut yarn. Using photo as a guide for placement and same end, sew Flower to Tote.

CUSHY PILLOW

EASY

Finished Size: 10" x 16"
(25.5 cm x 40.5 cm)

SHOPPING LIST

Yarn (Medium Weight) 4

[3 ounces, 197 yards
(85 grams, 180 meters) per skein]:

- ☐ Brown - 2 skeins
- ☐ Ecru Fleck - 1 skein
- ☐ Ecru - 1 skein
- ☐ Pink - 1 skein
- ☐ Rose - 1 skein

Crochet Hook

- ☐ Size I (5.5 mm)
  or size needed for gauge

Additional Supplies

- ☐ 10" x 16" (25.5 cm x 40.5 cm) pillow form

GAUGE INFORMATION

12 linked dc and 7 rows = 4" (10 cm)

Gauge Swatch: 4" (10 cm) square

Ch 14.

Rows 1-7: Work same as Back, page 22: 12 linked dc.

Finish off.

STITCH GUIDE

BEGINNING LINKED DOUBLE CROCHET ***(abbreviated beginning linked dc)***

Insert hook in second ch from hook, YO and pull up a loop, insert hook in first linked dc, YO and pull up a loop (3 loops on hook), (YO and draw through 2 loops on hook) twice.

LINKED DOUBLE CROCHET ***(abbreviated linked dc)***

Insert hook in horizontal bar of previous linked dc ***(Fig. A)***, YO and pull up a loop, insert hook in next st, YO and pull up a loop (3 loops on hook) ***(Fig. B)***, (YO and draw through 2 loops on hook) twice ***(Fig. C)***.

Fig. A

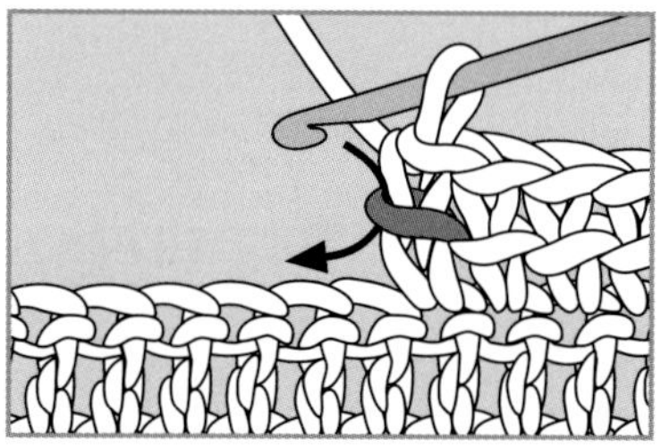

Fig. B

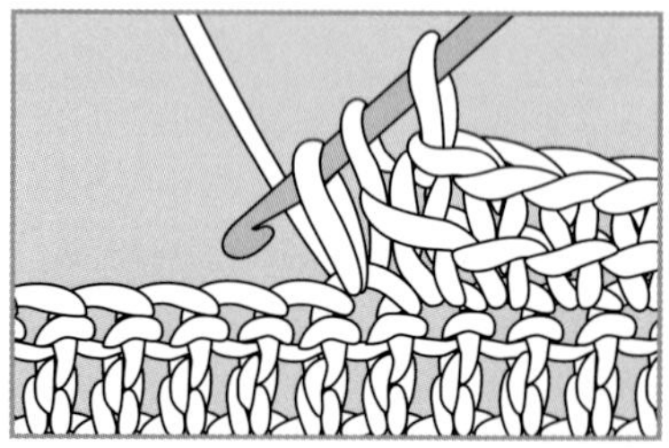

Fig. C

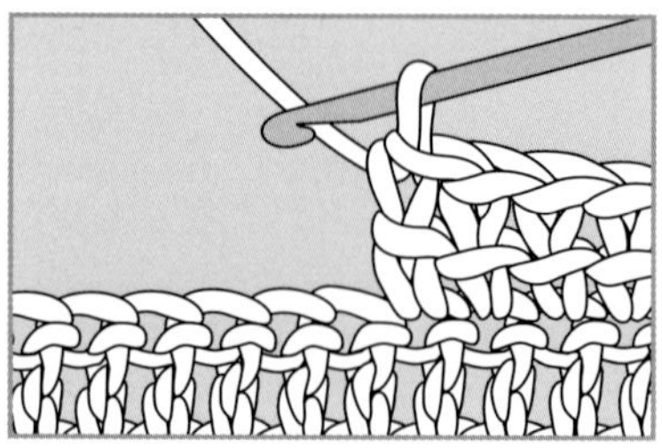

BACK

With Brown, ch 31, place marker in third ch from hook for st placement.

Row 1 (Right side)**:** Insert hook in second ch from hook, YO and pull up a loop, insert hook in marked ch, do **not** remove marker, YO and pull up a loop (3 loops on hook), (YO and draw through 2 loops on hook) twice **(counts as first linked dc)**, work linked dc across: 29 linked dc.

Note: Loop a short piece of yarn around any stitch to mark Row 1 as **right** side.

Rows 2-29: Ch 2, turn; work beginning linked dc, work linked dc across.

Do **not** finish off

TRIM

Ch 1, do **not** turn; work 46 sc evenly spaced across ends of rows; working in free loops of beginning ch ***(Fig. 2, page 29)***, 3 sc in first ch, sc in each ch across to marked ch, 3 sc in marked ch, remove marker; work 46 sc evenly spaced across ends of rows; 3 sc in first linked dc, sc in each linked dc across to last linked dc, 3 sc in last linked dc; join with slip st to first sc, finish off: 158 sc.

FRONT

With Brown, ch 31, place marker in third ch from hook for st placement.

Rows 1-8: Work same as Back: 29 linked dc.

Row 9: Ch 2, turn; work beginning linked dc, work linked dc across changing to Ecru Fleck in last linked dc ***(Fig. 3, page 29)***.

Rows 10-13: Ch 2, turn; work beginning linked dc, work linked dc across.

Row 14: Ch 2, turn; work beginning linked dc, work linked dc across changing to Ecru in last linked dc.

Rows 15-19: Repeat Rows 10-14 changing to Pink in last linked dc.

Rows 20-24: Repeat Rows 10-14 changing to Rose in last linked dc.

Rows 25-29: Repeat Rows 10-14 changing to Brown in last linked dc.

TRIM

Work same as Back.

FINISHING

With **wrong** sides together, Front facing, and working through inside loops only of **both** pieces, join Brown with sc in any sc ***(see Joining With Sc, page 29)***; sc in each sc around, inserting pillow form before closing; join with slip st to **both** loops of first sc, finish off.

LAP ROBE

●●○○ EASY

Finished Size: 31" x 49" (78.5 cm x124.5 cm)

Shown on page 24.

SHOPPING LIST

Yarn (Medium Weight) [4]

[5 ounces, 256 yards (141 grams, 234 meters) per skein]:

☐ White - 3 skeins

☐ Wine - 1 skein

☐ Green - 1 skein

[4 ounces, 212 yards (113 grams, 194 meters) per skein]:

☐ Grey - 1 skein

Crochet Hook

☐ Size H (5 mm) **or** size needed for gauge

GAUGE INFORMATION

Each Motif = 6½" (16.5 cm)

Gauge Swatch: 5" (12.75 cm) (from point to point)

Work same as Center: 66 sts and 6 ch-2 sps.

STITCH GUIDE

TREBLE CROCHET ***(abbreviated tr)***

YO twice, insert hook in st indicated, YO and pull up a loop (4 loops on hook), (YO and draw through 2 loops on hook) 3 times.

MOTIF

CENTER

(Make 10 Green, 9 Wine, 9 Grey, and 7 White)

With color indicated, ch 4; join with slip st to form a ring.

Rnd 1 (Right side)**:** (Ch 8, sc in ring) 6 times; do **not** join: 6 ch-8 sps.

Note: Loop a short piece of yarn around any stitch to mark Rnd 1 as **right** side.

Rnd 2: ★ (5 Sc, ch 2, 5 sc) in next ch-8 sp, slip st in next sc; repeat from ★ around, finish off: 66 sts and 6 ch-2 sps.

EDGING

Rnd 1: With **right** side facing, join White with sc in first ch-2 sp ***(see Joining With Sc, page 29)***, ch 4, skip next 5 sc, tr in next slip st, ch 4, skip next 5 sc, ★ sc in next ch-2 sp, ch 4, skip next 5 sc, tr in next slip st, ch 4, skip next 5 sc; repeat from ★ around; join with slip st to first sc: 12 sts and 12 ch-4 sps.

Rnd 2: Ch 6 **(counts as first dc plus ch 3, now and throughout)**, dc in same st as joining, 4 dc in next ch-4 sp, dc in next tr, 4 dc in next ch-4 sp, ★ (dc, ch 3, dc) in next sc, 4 dc in next ch-4 sp, dc in next tr, 4 dc in next ch-4 sp; repeat from ★ around; join with slip st to first dc, finish off: 66 dc and 6 ch-3 sps.

HALF MOTIF (Make 5)

With White, ch 4; join with slip st to form a ring.

Rnd 1 (Right side)**:** (Ch 8, sc in ring) 4 times; do **not** join: 4 sc and 4 ch-8 sps.

Note: Mark Rnd 1 as **right** side.

Rnd 2: ★ Sc in ring, (5 sc, ch 2, 5 sc) in next ch-8 sp, slip st in next sc; repeat from ★ 3 times **more**; finish off: 45 sts and 4 ch-2 sps.

Begin working in rows.

Row 1: With **right** side facing, join White with sc in first ch-2 sp; ★ ch 4, skip next 5 sc, tr in next slip st, ch 4, skip next 5 sc, sc in next ch-2 sp; repeat from ★ 2 times **more**, do **not** join and do **not** finish off: 7 sts and 6 ch-4 sps.

Last Rnd: Ch 6, dc in last sc made on Row 1 and in next 5 sc, skip next slip st, dc in next 6 sc, ★ (dc, ch 3, dc) in next sc, 4 dc in next ch-4 sp, dc in next tr, 4 dc in next ch-4 sp; repeat from ★ 2 times **more**; join with slip st to first dc, finish off: 46 dc and 4 ch-3 sps.

FINISHING

ASSEMBLY

Join Motifs as follows:
With **wrong** sides of two Motifs together and working through inside loops of sts on **both** pieces, join White with slip st in center ch of one ch-3 sp; slip st in each st across ending in center ch of next ch-3 sp; finish off.

Using Diagram as a guide for placement, join Motifs to form 5 vertical strips of 7 Motifs **each**, then join strips together in same manner. Join Half Motifs in spaces at end of each strip in same manner.

DIAGRAM

BORDER

Rnd 1: With **right** side facing, join White with slip st in ch-3 sp at Point A; ch 6, dc in same sp, dc in next 11 dc and in next ch, skip next seam, † dc in next ch and in next 11 dc, (dc, ch 3, dc) in next ch-3 sp, dc in next 11 dc and in next ch, skip next seam †; repeat from † to † 5 times **more**, dc in next ch and in next 11 dc, **[**(dc, ch 3, dc) in next ch-3 sp, dc in next 11 dc**]** twice, **[**working in same chs as seams across short edge, dc in next 4 chs and in 13 dc, dc in next 4 chs and in next 11 dc**]** twice, **[**(dc, ch 3, dc) in next ch-3 sp, dc in next 11 dc**]** twice, dc in next ch, skip next seam, repeat from † to † 6 times, dc in next ch and in next 11 dc, (dc, ch 3, dc) in next ch-3 sp, dc in next 12 dc, **[**working in same chs as seams across short edge, dc in next 4 chs and in next 11 dc, dc in next 4 chs and in next 13 dc**]** twice; join with slip st to first dc: 545 dc and 18 ch-3 sps.

Rnd 2: Slip st in next ch-3 sp, ch 6, dc in same sp, † dc in next 12 dc, skip next 2 dc, dc in next 12 dc, (dc, ch 3, dc) in next ch-3 sp; repeat from † to † 6 times **more**, dc in next 13 dc, (dc, ch 3, dc) in next ch-3 sp, working across short edge, dc in next dc and in each dc across to next ch-3 sp, (dc, ch 3, dc) in ch-3 sp, dc in next 13 dc, (dc, ch 3, dc) in next ch-3 sp, repeat from † to † 7 times, working across short edge, dc in next dc and in each dc across; join with slip st to first dc, finish off.

BED RUNNER

●●○○ EASY

Finished Size:

42" x 77" (106.5 cm x 195.5 cm)

SHOPPING LIST

Yarn (Medium Weight) MEDIUM 4

[4 ounces, 203 yards (113 grams, 186 meters) per skein]:

- ☐ Peach - 2 skeins
- ☐ Green - 2 skeins
- ☐ Taupe - 2 skeins
- ☐ Cream - 2 skeins

Crochet Hook

- ☐ Size J (6 mm) **or** size needed for gauge

GAUGE INFORMATION

In pattern, (V-St, Puff St) twice and 5 rows = 4" (10 cm)

Gauge Swatch: 5¾"w x 4"h (14.5 cm x 10 cm)

With Cream, ch 20.

Rows 1-5: Work same as Body: 3 V-Sts and 2 Puff Sts.

Finish off.

STITCH GUIDE

V-STITCH ***(abbreviated V-St)***

(Dc, ch 2, dc) in stitch indicated.

PUFF STITCH ***(abbreviated Puff St)***

(uses one st or sp)

★ YO, insert hook in st or sp indicated, YO and pull up a loop even with loop on hook; repeat from ★ 2 times **more**, YO and draw through all 7 loops on hook, ch 1 to close.

BODY

With Peach, ch 128.

Row 1 (Right side)**:** Working in back ridges of beginning ch ***(Fig. 1, page 29)***, work V-St in sixth ch from hook **(first 4 skipped chs count as first dc plus ch 1)**, ★ skip next 2 chs, work Puff St in next ch, skip next 2 chs, work V-St in next ch; repeat from ★ across to last 2 chs, ch 1, skip next ch, dc in last ch: 21 V-Sts and 20 Puff Sts.

Note: Loop a short piece of yarn around any stitch to mark Row 1 as **right** side.

Row 2: Ch 3 **(counts as first dc, now and throughout)**, turn; work Puff St in next V-St (ch-2 sp), ★ work V-St in top of next Puff St, work Puff St in next V-St; repeat from ★ across, dc in last dc: 20 V-sts and 21 Puff Sts.

Row 3: Ch 3, turn; work V-St in top of next Puff St, ★ work Puff St in next V-St, work V-St in next Puff St; repeat from ★ across, dc in last dc: 21 V-Sts and 20 Puff Sts.

Rows 4-11: Repeat Rows 2 and 3, 4 times.

Row 12: Ch 3, turn; work Puff St in next V-St, ★ work V-St in top of next Puff St, work Puff St in next V-St; repeat from ★ across, dc in last dc changing to Green ***(Fig. 3, page 29)***; cut Peach.

Row 13: Ch 3, turn; work V-St in top of next Puff St, ★ work Puff St in next V-St, work V-St in next Puff St; repeat from ★ across, dc in last dc changing to Peach; cut Green.

Rows 14-96: Repeat Rows 2 and 3 for pattern, working in following stripe sequence: 1 Row Peach, 12 rows Green, 1 row Taupe, 1 row Green, 12 rows Taupe, 1 row Cream, 1 row Taupe, 12 rows Cream, 1 row Taupe, 1 row Cream, 12 rows Taupe, 1 row Green, 1 row Taupe, 12 rows Green, 1 row Peach, 1 row Green, 12 rows Peach.

Finish off.

GENERAL INSTRUCTIONS

ABBREVIATIONS

BPdc	Back Post double crochet(s)	LDC	Long Double Crochet(s)
ch(s)	chain(s)	mm	millimeters
cm	centimeters	Rnd(s)	Round(s)
dc	double crochet(s)	sc	single crochet(s)
FPdc	Front Post double crochet(s)	sp(s)	space(s)
		st(s)	stitch(es)
hdc	half double crochet(s)	tr	treble crochet(s)
hdc2tog	half double crochet 2 together	YO	yarn over

SYMBOLS & TERMS

★ — work instructions following ★ as many **more** times as indicated in addition to the first time.

† to † — work all instructions from first † to second † **as many** times as specified.

( ) or [ ] — work enclosed instructions **as many** times as specified by the number immediately following **or** work all enclosed instructions in the stitch or space indicated **or** contains explanatory remarks.

colon (:) — the number(s) given after a colon at the end of a row or round denote(s) the number of stitches and spaces you should have on that row or round.

Yarn Weight Symbol & Names	LACE 0	SUPER FINE 1	FINE 2	LIGHT 3	MEDIUM 4	BULKY 5	SUPER BULKY 6	JUMBO 7
Type of Yarns in Category	Fingering, size 10 crochet thread	Sock, Fingering, Baby	Sport, Baby	DK, Light Worsted	Worsted, Afghan, Aran	Chunky, Craft, Rug	Super Bulky, Roving	Jumbo, Roving
Crochet Gauge* Ranges in Single Crochet to 4" (10 cm)	32-42 sts**	21-32 sts	16-20 sts	12-17 sts	11-14 sts	8-11 sts	6-9 sts	5 sts and fewer
Advised Hook Size Range	Steel*** 6 to 8, Regular hook B-1	B-1 to E-4	E-4 to 7	7 to I-9	I-9 to K-10½	K-10½ to M/N-13	M/N-13 to Q	Q and larger

*GUIDELINES ONLY: The chart above reflects the most commonly used gauges and hook sizes for specific yarn categories.

** Lace weight yarns are usually crocheted with larger hooks to create lacy openwork patterns. Accordingly, a gauge range is difficult to determine. Always follow the gauge stated in your pattern.

*** Steel crochet hooks are sized differently from regular hooks–the higher the number, the smaller the hook, which is the reverse of regular hook sizing.

CROCHET TERMINOLOGY		
UNITED STATES		INTERNATIONAL
slip stitch (slip st)	=	single crochet (sc)
single crochet (sc)	=	double crochet (dc)
half double crochet (hdc)	=	half treble crochet (htr)
double crochet (dc)	=	treble crochet (tr)
treble crochet (tr)	=	double treble crochet (dtr)
double treble crochet (dtr)	=	triple treble crochet (ttr)
triple treble crochet (tr tr)	=	quadruple treble crochet (qtr)
skip	=	miss

●○○○ **BEGINNER**	Projects for first-time crocheters using basic stitches. Minimal shaping.
●●○○ **EASY**	Projects using yarn with basic stitches, repetitive stitch patterns, simple color changes, and simple shaping and finishing.
●●●○ **INTERMEDIATE**	Projects using a variety of techniques, such as basic lace patterns or color patterns, mid-level shaping and finishing.
●●●● **EXPERIENCED**	Projects with intricate stitch patterns, techniques and dimension, such as non-repeating patterns, multi-color techniques, fine threads, small hooks, detailed shaping and refined finishing.

CROCHET HOOKS																	
U.S.	B-1	C-2	D-3	E-4	F-5	G-6	7	H-8	I-9	J-10	K-10½	L-11	M/N-13	N/P-15	P/Q	Q	S
Metric - mm	2.25	2.75	3.25	3.5	3.75	4	4.5	5	5.5	6	6.5	8	9	10	15	16	19

GAUGE

Exact gauge is **essential** for proper size. Before beginning your project, make the sample swatch given in the individual instructions in the yarn and hook specified. After completing the swatch, measure it, counting your stitches and rows/rounds carefully. If your swatch is larger or smaller than specified, **make another, changing hook size to get the correct gauge**. Keep trying until you find the size hook that will give you the specified gauge.

JOINING WITH SC

When instructed to join with sc, begin with a slip knot on hook. Insert hook in stitch or space indicated, YO and pull up a loop, YO and draw through both loops on hook.

JOINING WITH DC

When instructed to join with dc, begin with a slip knot on hook. YO, holding loop on hook, insert hook in stitch or space indicated, YO and pull up a loop (3 loops on hook), (YO and draw through 2 loops on hook) twice.

BACK RIDGE

Work only in loops indicated by arrows ***(Fig. 1)***.

Fig. 1

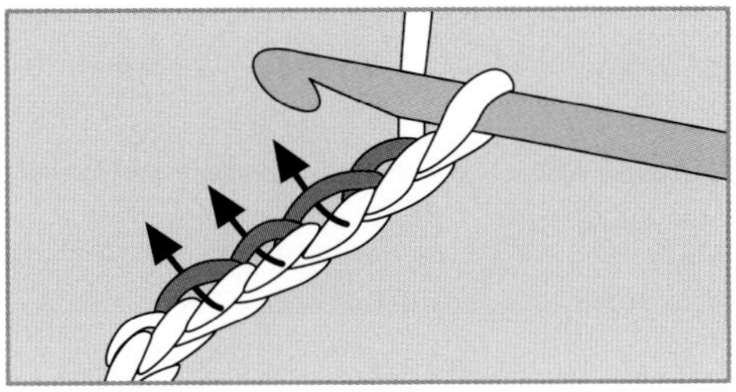

FREE LOOPS OF A CHAIN

When instructed to work in free loops of a chain, work in loop indicated by arrow ***(Fig. 2)***.

Fig. 2

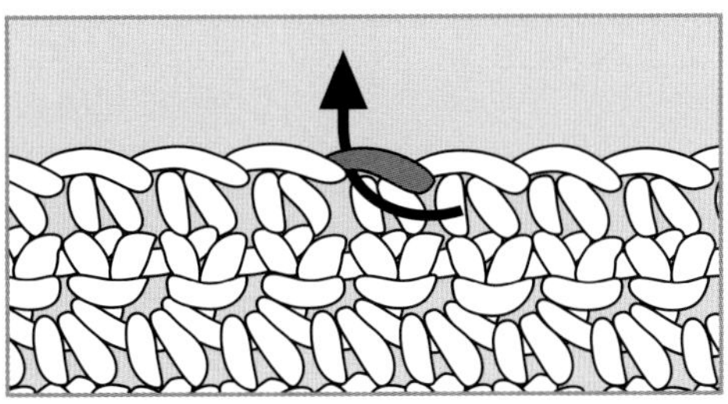

CHANGING COLORS

YO, insert hook in stitch indicated, YO and pull up a loop, YO and draw through 2 loops on hook, drop yarn, with new yarn ***(Fig. 3)***, YO and draw through 2 loops on hook.

Fig. 3

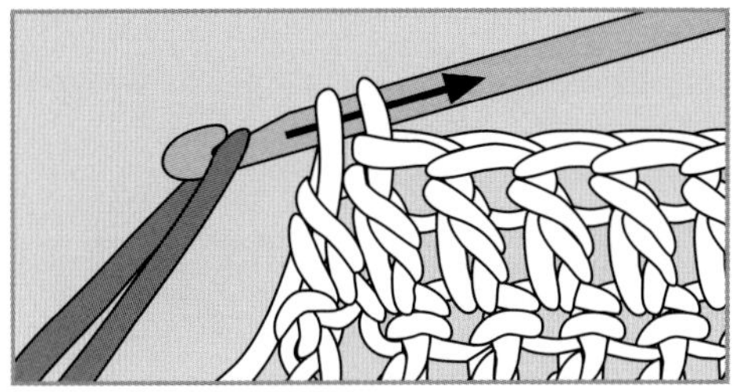

POST STITCH

Work around post of stitch indicated, inserting hook in direction of arrow ***(Fig. 4)***.

Fig. 4

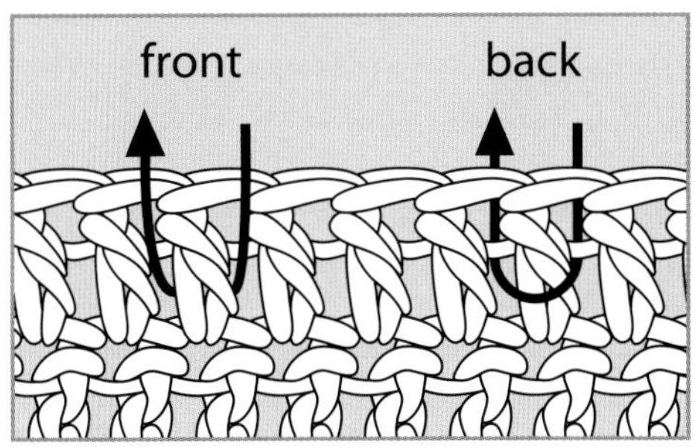

REVERSE SINGLE CROCHET

(abbreviated reverse sc)

Working from **left** to **right**, ★ insert hook in stitch to right of hook ***(Fig. 5a)***, YO and draw through, under and to left of loop on hook (2 loops on hook) ***(Fig. 5b)***, YO and draw through both loops on hook ***(Fig. 5c)*** **(reverse sc made, *Fig. 5d*)**; repeat from ★ around.

Fig. 5a

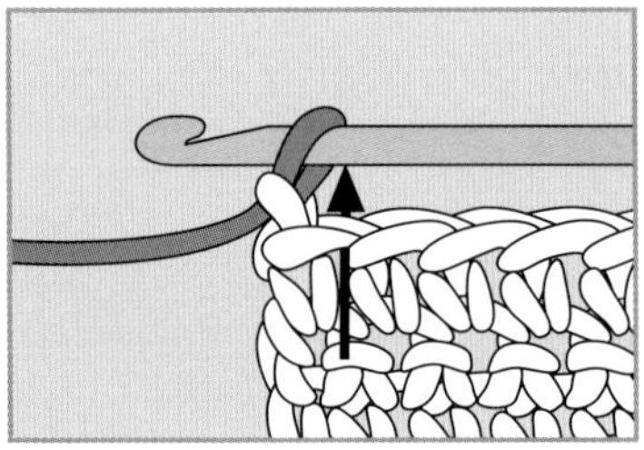

Fig. 5b

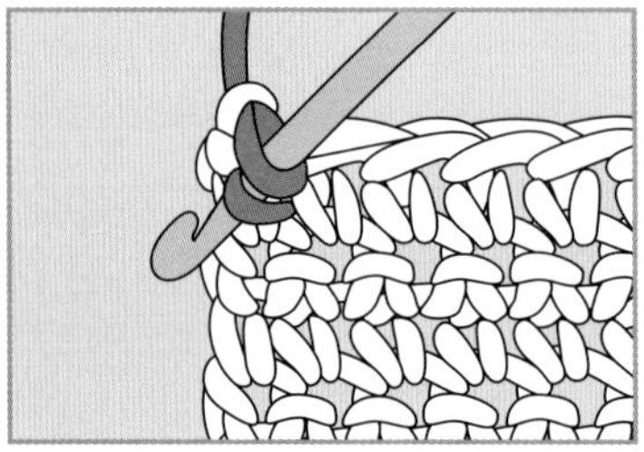

Fig. 5c

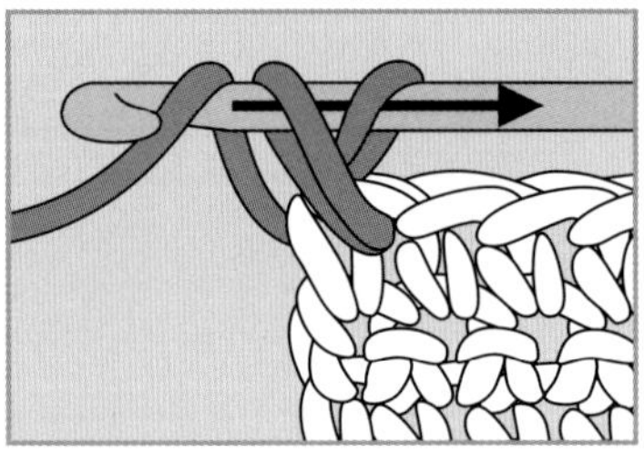

Fig. 5d

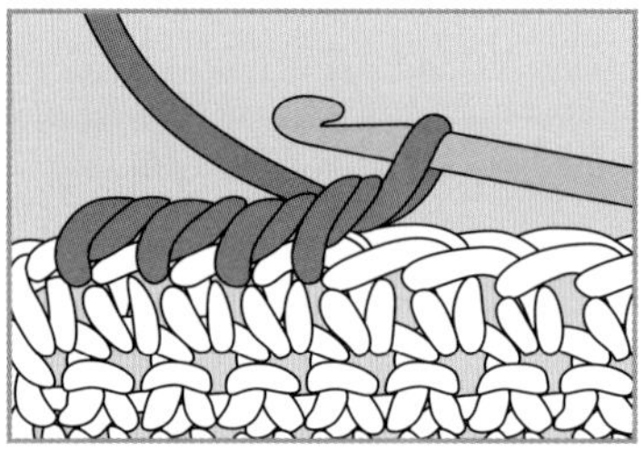

WORKING IN SPACE BEFORE A STITCH

When instructed to work in space **before** a stitch or in spaces **between** stitches, insert hook in space indicated by arrow ***(Fig. 6)***.

Fig. 6

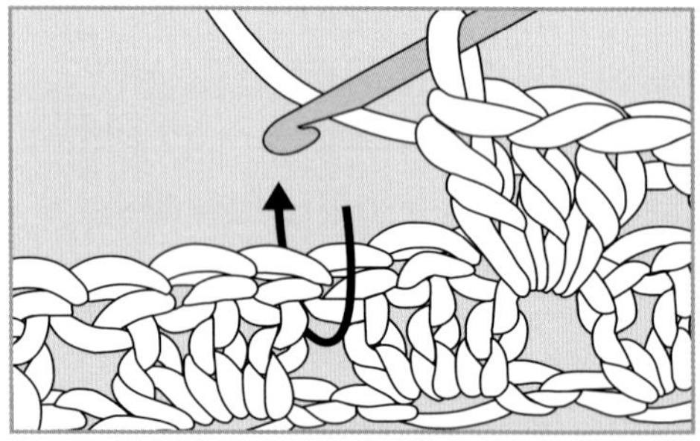

WORKING AROUND A STITCH

Work in stitch or space indicated, inserting hook in direction of arrow ***(Fig. 7)***.

Fig. 7

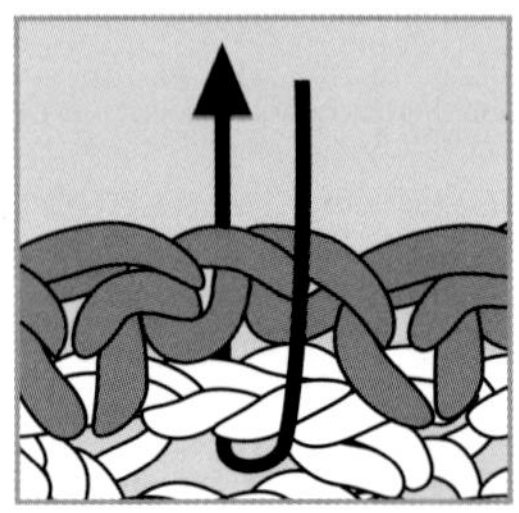

YARN INFORMATION

Each item in this book was made using either Medium Weight or Light Weight Yarn. Any brand of the specifed weight of yarn may be used. It is best to refer to the yardage/meters when determining how many balls or skeins to purchase. Remember, to arrive at the finished size, it is the GAUGE/TENSION that is important, not the brand of yarn.

For your convenience, listed below are the specific yarns used to create our photography models. Because yarn manufacturers make frequent changes to their product lines, you may sometimes find it necessary to use a substitute yarn or to search for the discontinued product at alternate suppliers (locally or online).

LACY WRAP
Lion Brand® New Basic 175
Grey - #152 Charcoal
Cream - #098 Cream
Pink - #101 Peony

SIMPLE SCARF
Lion Brand® Mandala®
#215 Warlock

STAR BLANKET
Lion Brand® New Basic 175
Black - #153 Black
Green - #172 Grass
Lt Grey - #150 Grey
Dk Grey - #152 Charcoal
Cream - #098 Cream

SLOUCHY HAT
Premier® DYI Gradient Yarn Box
#1046-08 Water

TRIANGLE SHAWL
Bernat® Pop!™
#84008 Moonshadow

SWEET TOTE
Red Heart® Super Saver® Ombre™
#3968 Purple

CUSHY PILLOW
Lion Brand® Wool-Ease®
Brown - #403 Mushroom
Ecru Fleck - #402 Wheat
Ecru - #098 Natural Heather
Pink - #104 Blush Heather
Rose - #140 Rose Heather

LAP ROBE
Red Heart® Soft®
White - #4600 White
Wine - #3729 Grape
Green - #9870 Deep Sea
Grey - #9440 Lt Grey Heather

BED RUNNER
Premier® Yarns Deborah Norville Everyday® Soft Worsted Solids
Peach - #100-55 Soft Peach
Green - #100-51 Spa
Taupe - #100-52 Chinchilla
Cream - #100-02 Cream

MEET KRISTI SIMPSON

Inspired by her love of yarn, Kristi Simpson enjoys creating crochet and knit patterns with a fresh and modern touch.

The mother of five became hooked on crochet after teaching herself so she could help her daughter make a scarf from a "learn to crochet" kit that was a gift.

"I loved it from the beginning," she says. "I was amazed that I could take a string of yarn and create something so useful and pretty! Needless to say, I never stopped!"

Her designs have been published in several books and more than 50 magazine features. To see more of her designs, visit kristisimpson.net or find her on Ravelry, Facebook, and Pinterest.

Production Team: Instructional/ Technical Editor - Sarah J. Green; Editorial Writer - Susan Frantz Wiles; Senior Graphic Artist - Lora Puls; Graphic Artists - Kytanna McFarlin and Leia Morshedi; Photo Stylist - Lori Wenger; and Photographer - Jason Masters.